*This book is dedicated
to my dear friend, Jane.*

*Always in my heart and memories.
'Thanks for all the adventures!'*

With much love, Mel x

CONTENTS

Introducing Mel Pross
On her journey to EnRich mind body & spirit

Dear Readers,

Welcome, and thank you for joining me for this little escape where you'll find a treasured collection of my poetry, inspirational messages and photography.

Many people ask, 'What inspired your poetry?' Well, that requires a little peek into my life journey so far...

As a young, sensitive child, I was often drawn to natural environments — day dreaming and gazing at wildlife and the sky. I would often find myself questioning - What is life? What is consciousness? What is... 'IS'? What followed was a passion for researching, exploring and learning anything about nature, the cosmos, the Universe.

Years later, I went through a period of deep, self-review. During the healing process, I tapped into many of the skills and knowledge I had acquired throughout my life - which included daily meditations and long, solitary treks through countryside.

What happened next was amazing!

My inquisitive mind came alive again. I regained my intense love of nature, but from a much deeper perspective – with a true sense of connection to all things.

I was reminded of who I truly am!6

As I grew stronger and more enriched, I began documenting my experiences by taking photographs, creating art work, and... writing!

This book is a collection of my poetry, photographs and art work, and is part of a larger Project of creative works - including my main book of personal philosophies, inspirational messages and meditations.

It's a real pleasure to have you join my journey and hope that you find my poetry a joy, a comfort and an inspiration.

With much love, Mel Pross x

EnRich

mind * body * spirit

Find me on Facebook, Instagram and You Tube at
'Mel Pross, EnRichmbs'

A Gentle Touch

A gentle touch
Of empathy and love
At just the right moment
Says more than a thousand words.

A Vision of Love

And there it was,
A vision of Love.
Bewitched me!
And I was taken!
Both lost and found.

An Empath's Tale

All those in pain – I feel you
All those in fear – I comfort you
All those in sadness – I hold you.

All those in joy
I shine with you
All those in laughter
I sing with you
All those in Love
I Love You.

And Peace Reigned Eternal

And there she was! Across the cosmic web.
A unicorn of purple, that glowed like the golden sun.
He saw her and, for the first time, felt alive.
And, in that instant,
All his dreams came true.

And there he was! Across the cosmic field.
A stallion of black, that blazed like burning embers.
She saw him and at once felt safe.
And, in that instant,
All her dreams came true.

And so it was, that they could be apart no more.
And, upon that thought, instantly, they were entwined
Til their hearts beat as one,
And peace reigned eternal.

As Love Replaces Fear

When subside the pain and fear,
And mists of confusion start to clear,
Allow love's light to filter through,
To re-harmonise the inner you.
Then the gentle, kind and true,
Steadily and faithfully
Will come to you,

As Love replaces fear.

As She Sleeps

And as she sleeps
So does the dragon
As she awakens,

Fire !

Take to the skies,
Dear, glorious Goddess,
And with the dragon's Magick
Create pure beings of Light
Who, to you,

Do truly aspire.

Be Still

If you want to hear,
Be silent.

If you want to see,
Close your eyes.

If you want to feel,
Be still.

By Her Fingertips

By her fingertips, she clung
To every piece of wisdom found
Within each hurt, pain, fear, dark cloud,
And immersed herself in Love's sweet sound
Til every heartbeat sang!
And heart and mind, once more,
Were One.

Could It Be

Could it be that we
Are not He, She or Me,
But one giant ball of energy,
Spiralling eternally,
Evolving relentlessly,
One consciousness, one reality?

That we are not apart,
But each a vital part
Of one true heart,
All feeling,
All seeing,
As One colossal Being?

Could it be
That, finally,
We will see,
That I am You,
And You
Are Me?

Do You

If only you could...

See the beauty of nature, as I do
Feel the comfort of nature, as I do
Hear the joy of nature, as I do
Be the love of nature, as I do

But wait – you can!

Do you?

Dusk

Each day...

There are few, precious moments
Where nature holds its breath
And consciousness hovers
Between two worlds.

Even In The Darkness

Even in the darkness,
Somewhere
The sun shines ever brightly.
Keep your love light burning,
To light the way
For those in darkness.

With all my heart and soul
I share my deepest love,
To heal, to comfort,
To hold your hand
And, into the future,
Together, we will go.

F r e   e

On this day

In this moment

I am free.

From My Dark Sleep

As I re-emerged from my dark sleep
I realised that She had been there all along

Piercing through the darkness
With her unshakeable, golden brilliance.

Yes – She was still there.
All I had to do...

Was open my eyes!

Gaze Deeply

Gaze deeply

Into my eyes

And you will find

The Universe.

Her Smiles

Her smiles may hide the fear
Inside, so do not mock or sneer,
But support and hold her near,
To show that you will always be here,
And forever love each other dear.

Her True Self

As the sea of tears subsided,
She wiped away the tears
To find herself gazing out at the world
Through child's eyes,
And realised it was her own child Self.
Her true Self.

And, despite the years that had passed,
With all their dramas,
SHE had not changed.
She was still she.

And, for all her seeking,
Her questioning and her doubts,
The answers were within her all along!
Unchanged...

And, finally, she knew
Her True Self.

hush

The storm raged,
And fought to tear her down.

But the Willow merely swayed,
And bent her gentle limbs,

And hushed its wicked whispers
With her song.

I Am Home

At first, I'd look up at the birds
And yearn to fly.
Then I'd look up at the clouds
And yearn to touch the sky.

Now, I gaze up at the sun,
The moon and stars
And know, that,
Wherever I may be,

I am Home.

I Am You

Deep within mind... I know you.

Deep within my heart... I feel you.

Deep within my soul... I am you.

I Await You

With joy ... I await you.

With warmth ... I feel you.

With grace ... I come to you.

With love... I embrace you.

I Love You

Whoever you are …
I care about you.
What you've done …
I forgive you.
Whatever your struggles …
I support you.
Whatever your sadness …
I comfort you.
Whatever your fears …
I hold you.

Whenever you care about me,
Forgive me, support me,
Comfort, respect and hold me …
I appreciate you.
Whenever you love me…
I love you.

Is There a Place?

Is there a place

Outside time and space

Where reside our states,

Of mind and grace?

Isle
of
Avalon

Vibrant auras,
Secret places,
Tree bark forming wise, old faces.

Whispers fill the morning air,
Shadows startle!
But there's no-one there.

Never is the sun more golden,
Never am I more beholden

Magical, mystical, Isle of Avalon,
Embrace me!
Leave me not alone!

Isle of Avalon

I cannot go!
I cannot leave!
Webs of intrigue forever weave
Around me silken, love's sweet chains.

So homesick never will I be ... Again.

Magick

So young and so pure,
There is no concept of magick,
Since, to her,
Everything is possible!

Make Your Journey

Make your journey
Keep going!
Even if the way ahead is unclear
Follow your heart...

...and it will take you
Home.

MAKE
YOUR
WISH

Put aside all anger, greed and envy,
And reach inside your soul.
Then make your wish!
And surrender to the Universe!

NATURE BECOMES ME

WALKING INTO THE WOODS
I ENTER ANOTHER DIMENSION
AND THEN I STOP – AND RECEIVE
AND NATURE BECOMES ME.

Once Seen

Cannot be unseen

Once Spoken – cannot be unspoken

Once Known – cannot be unknown

Tread softly, humbly
And respectfully
Into the Wilderness.

She

She never sleeps,
Never lazing.
Ever watching, ever blazing.

Everything you say, she hears.
Everything you do, she feels.

All your questions and debating,
All this while she keeps creating.

Not a flicker, not a flaw,
She's everything you need,
And more!

I am her,
And she is me.

Love and Light Eternally.

She Turned
And Faced The Darkness

So She turned
And faced the Darkness,
And stared and stared,
'Til, eventually,
She saw the Light.

The More I Look

The more I look,
The more I see,

And what at first appears empty,
Is really a whole new world – a sea
Of new realities,
In front of me,
Around me,
A part of me.

The more I look,
The more I see.

The Roots of Your Past

Let the roots of your past anchor you.

Fully embrace and express the present.

Reach out with Love to the future.

The Sky Wept

The sky wept and wept,
Til, finally,
The clouds parted,

And opened
Was the heavenly eye,
That beamed its golden smile
both far and wide.

The Earthlings gasped!
For, surely, those were tears of joy all along!

The Wise One

'Who?'   'YOU'   said The Wise One.

'How?'   'DO'   said The Wise One.

'When?'   'NOW'   said The Wise One.

Time To Listen

The Universe is calling me;
Time to listen.

If you want to hear,
Be still.

Tread Softly

Through the Darkness shines the Light,
Revealing all that's good and right.

As Lightness does protect the shade,
Where dreams, ideas
And fantasies are made.

Tread softly through the crystal maze,
And with compassion, love
And tenderness,

End your days.

Try

Try

Again

Step back
Through the mists of pain
and confusion.

Step back
With empathy, compassion
and Love.

Then try again
With honesty, integrity, respect;
With an open heart,

And all need not be lost.
But new and stronger trust
Be the foundation of
a greater bond
Than ever there was before.

Walk In The Woods

Through the woods,

The trees whisper their secrets

The birds rejoice in their song

The squirrels laugh

And play hide 'n' seek

and harmony is Home.

With My Tears

And, with my tears, springs forth a river
To ease the rocky way,
To cleanse your hurt and pain,
To energise your spirit
And feed your heart again,
And support you on your journey...

Your special journey of Love.

Yes

The glorious sun bursting through
The majestic trees,
Yes

The wind whispering its secrets
Through the leaves,
Yes

Apple blossom
Nodding gently
in the breeze,

Yes,

   Yes,

      Yes.

You

Are

Wiser than you think,

Braver than you feel,

More loved

Than you will ever know.

The following 4 bonus poems...

*...were written during the challenging times
of the year 2020.*

*Reflecting inner fears, but also the hope, love and
support shown around the world, these poems
were manifested following my sustained, deep
meditation, prayers and reflection.*

Sending Love out to the Universe,

Mel Pross

Lost and Found

Lost in the labyrinth of her own mind,
She scurries through the twists and turns
Of ifs and whats and whys,
All senses reaching overload.

Clutching her head in despair,
Moments before it explodes into oblivion,
Vanished is her spine!
And, as a ragdoll,
She drops to the ground,
The hard, stoney ground,
In submission and surrender,
And darkness is peace.

But then, behold, the Earth relents.
It gives, it envelopes,
It embraces her pain,
Easing the strain,
Soothing the mind, and
Hushing the panic and fear.

And the turbulence that once ripped her apart,
Now rocks her gently as a babe,
'Til darkness is filled with rainbow light,
And all that was
Lost is Found.

My Truth

As I ever onward tread,
Sweet meadow kisses under naked feet
Caress my fragile soul,
And lift my mind to greater thoughts;
Of love and tenderness,
Nurtured from within my throbbing heart,
That aches and yearns to heal for ever
The loneliness, the pain.
To bring to shore the abandoned driftwood,
Glinting under the solar flare,
Bobbing alone in the voidal vastness.

Yet, with each step, behold, I grow,
I transform, one particle at a time.
Until, at last, a golden glow
Like angel wings,
Expanding from inside of me,
Outwards, upwards, in all dimensions,
Consumes all darkness.

And, finally, I see that I am truly part of
The Whole, The One, The Eternal.
That I shine as brightly as the sun,
And in my transcendent astonishment,
I smile, I accept,
And step confidently into
My Truth.

Sweet Love

Sweet Love Embrace me!
Hold me tight
Till forever is but a distant
memory.

Whisper of Hope

An anomalous blend of dread and exaltation
Leaks no insight into atop what I stand.
Be it, below, some strange, unfamiliar land,
Or conundrum, this long lost soul of mine
Had eons ago planned.

What rocky form is this,
Upon which I teeter between rise and fall?
A speck of sand, a stone, a mountain,
Or nothing at all?

Except that whisper of hope
That plays tug o' war with my doubt.
And when all is done, it's done.
Over
And Out.

Acknowledgements

I'd like to thank
all the special people in my life, both present and departed,
who have nurtured me, supported me, pushed me, inspired me
and, above all else, loved me.
For all of these experiences, in some way, large or small,
have inspired me in my writings.
Sending Love, Mel x

Credits

'hush - and other poems' by Mel Pross
AUTHOR, ARTIST, PHILOSOPHER
Poetry, images & art work written and created by Mel Pross
©EnRich mind body spirit (aka EnRichmbs)

Design Credits:
www.canva.com - design platform
Lauren L Pross - Marketing Design Consultant

Contact Details:

Follow MEL PROSS on her journey to
EnRich mind, body & spirit
#melsjourney   Email: enrichmbs@gmail.com

EnRich
*mind * body * spirit*

Printed in Great Britain
by Amazon